# Looking at . . . Ceratosaurus

## A Dinosaur from the JURASSIC Period

Weekly Reader®
BOOKS

Published by arrangement with Gareth Stevens, Inc.
Newfield Publications is a federally registered trademark
of Newfield Publications, Inc. Weekly Reader is a federally
registered trademark of Weekly Reader Corporation.

**Library of Congress Cataloging-in-Publication Data**

Brown, Mike, 1947-
   Looking at-- Ceratosaurus/written by Mike Brown; illustrated by Tony Gibbons.
     p. cm. -- (The New dinosaur collection)
   Includes index.
   ISBN 0-8368-1138-0
   1. Ceratosaurus--Juvenile literature. [1. Ceratosaurus. 2. Dinosaurs.] I. Gibbons, Tony, ill.
II. Title. III. Series.
QE862.S3B764  1994
567.9'7--dc20                             94-11523

This North American edition first published in 1994 by
**Gareth Stevens Publishing**
1555 North RiverCenter Drive, Suite 201
Milwaukee, Wisconsin  53212  USA

This U.S. edition © 1994 by Gareth Stevens, Inc.  Created with original © 1994 by
Quartz Editorial Services, Premier House, 112 Station Road, Edgware HA8 7AQ U.K.

Consultant: Dr. David Norman, Director of the Sedgwick Museum of Geology,
University of Cambridge, England.

Additional artwork by Clare Herronneau.

Printed in the United States of America

Weekly Reader Books Presents

# Looking at . . . Ceratosaurus

## A Dinosaur from the JURASSIC Period

by Mike Brown

Illustrated by Tony Gibbons

THE NEW
DINOSAUR
COLLECTION

Gareth Stevens Publishing
MILWAUKEE

# Contents

5    Introducing **Ceratosaurus**

6    Horned lizard

8    A hunter's skeleton

10   In Late Jurassic times

12   Killer carnivore

14   Horned fighter

16   Dinosaur footprints

18   Great **Ceratosaurus** mysteries

20   **Ceratosaurus** data

22   Meet some other carnivores

24   Glossary and Index

# Introducing
# Ceratosaurus

If human beings had existed 150 million years ago, you might have been able to go dinosaur-spotting. And perhaps you would have come across a **Ceratosaurus** (SER-A-TOE-SAW-RUS).

You would probably have been terrified!

There are many puzzling things about **Ceratosaurus**. What, for instance, was the purpose of that horn on its snout? Why did it have one more finger than most large meat-eaters? And why did it have a ridge down its back?

Let's find out what it would have been like to come face-to-face with **Ceratosaurus**.

You would have had to keep your distance, though – for this was a fierce, meat-eating dinosaur. It had a horn on its snout and bony ridges over its eyes.

5

# Horned lizard

It would have been easy to recognize **Ceratosaurus** because it had a rather special feature. Its snout had a large, bony horn – a little like the horn of a rhinoceros.

This big bump is what gives this dinosaur its name, meaning "horned lizard." It was given this name by the famous American paleontologist, O. C. Marsh. Sharp, bony ridges over the eyes would also have made **Ceratosaurus** easy to identify.

Ceratosaurus was a strongly built animal. It was almost as long as a bus and well over 6.5 feet (2 meters) tall. This dinosaur was designed for hunting. Its head was large compared with the rest of the body, and it used its powerful jaws to grab hold of prey and tear off chunks of meat.

The jaws were filled with long, sharp teeth that were curved inward. When Ceratosaurus held a struggling animal in its mouth, the victim could not escape, try as it might.

Another feature of this dinosaur was the low, jagged ridge of bony plates that ran down the middle of its back.

Ceratosaurus also had a deep and broad tail that helped it keep its balance as it traveled over the plains or through Jurassic forests.

Ceratosaurus certainly seems to have been an ugly brute and was probably as fierce as it looked. What a roar it must have made!

The list that follows is your spotter's guide to identifying a Ceratosaurus.

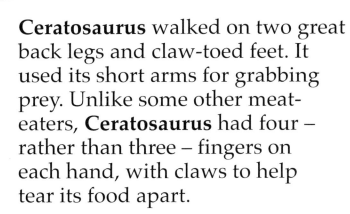

Ceratosaurus walked on two great back legs and claw-toed feet. It used its short arms for grabbing prey. Unlike some other meat-eaters, Ceratosaurus had four – rather than three – fingers on each hand, with claws to help tear its food apart.

- a large, bony horn on the snout
- powerful jaws and sharp teeth
- four-fingered hands and short arms
- a low ridge down its back
- a body as long as a bus

What a strange-looking, colossal creature Ceratosaurus was!

# A hunter's skeleton

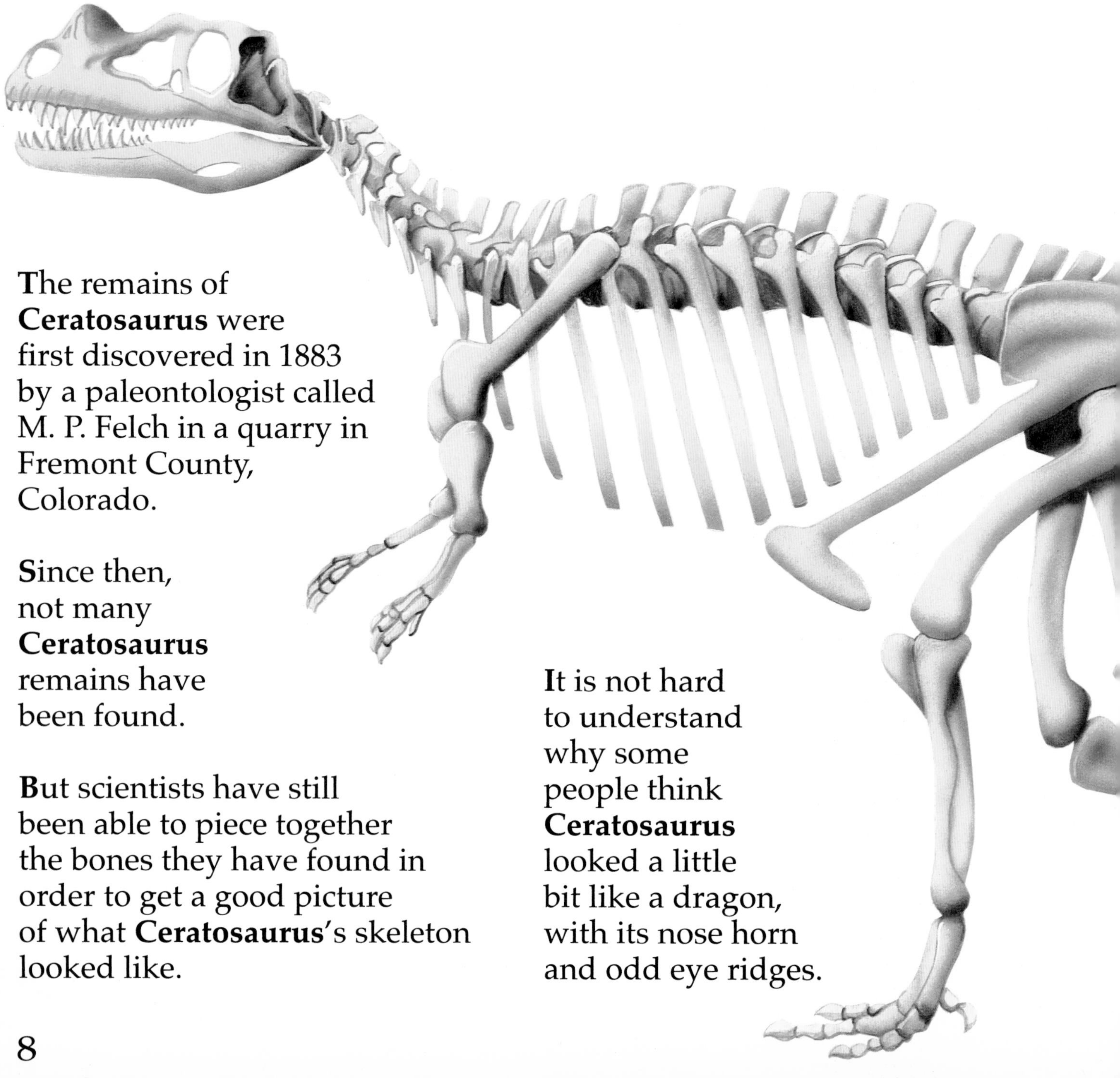

The remains of
**Ceratosaurus** were
first discovered in 1883
by a paleontologist called
M. P. Felch in a quarry in
Fremont County,
Colorado.

Since then,
not many
**Ceratosaurus**
remains have
been found.

But scientists have still
been able to piece together
the bones they have found in
order to get a good picture
of what **Ceratosaurus**'s skeleton
looked like.

It is not hard
to understand
why some
people think
**Ceratosaurus**
looked a little
bit like a dragon,
with its nose horn
and odd eye ridges.

8

But the skeleton of **Ceratosaurus** is actually that of a well-designed hunter and meat-eater. Look, for instance, at its head.

Its skull was quite large, and most of it consisted of jaws that were even bigger than those of a larger creature – **Allosaurus** (AL-OH-SAW-RUS).

To keep it lightweight, **Ceratosaurus**'s skull was not solid bone; instead, it was filled with large spaces.

**Ceratosaurus**'s neck was fairly short and straight, as you can see in this picture. But there would have been powerful muscles in the neck. **Ceratosaurus** needed these to hold up its head.

The bones of **Ceratosaurus**'s hips were quite unusual. From its remains, scientists can see that they were firmly joined together, almost as if in one piece.

Take a look at **Ceratosaurus**'s legs and compare them with the length of its arms. What a difference! Those powerful legs had to support a very heavy body.

From the tip of its snout to the tip of its tail, **Ceratosaurus** measured about 20 feet (6 m) long.

Scientists have also noticed from its remains that **Ceratosaurus** seems to have had a low ridge of upright bony plates down the middle of its back.

The fact that not many remains of **Ceratosaurus** have been found has led some scientists to believe that they probably did not live in large groups. Instead, they may have preferred to live in small families, or even alone.

# In Late Jurassic times

**Ceratosaurus** lived during the Late Jurassic Period in parts of the world now known as western North America and East Africa. During that time, the days were mild and rainy. Giant forests grew along riverbanks and coasts.

Among the most common plants were stumpy cycads, delicate ferns, and tall conifers.

Scientists believe that, in North America, **Ceratosaurus** stalked a low-lying plain that rested between the Rocky Mountains and a vast inland sea.

Here, beside the lagoons and mud banks, were many other kinds of dinosaurs, too. Most were plant-eaters, such as the huge, long-necked, long-tailed **Diplodocus** (DIP-LOD-OH-KUS) and plated **Stegosaurus** (STEG-OH-SAW-RUS).

There were other meat-eaters, too, such as fearsome **Allosaurus** (AL-OH-SAW-RUS) and the much smaller **Ornitholestes** (OR-NITH-OH-LESS-TEEZ), a lightly-built, fast-running hunter. How many of these dinosaurs can you spot in this picture?

11

# Killer carnivore

**Ceratosaurus** must have spent much of its time searching for food. It was a fairly large carnivore and needed plenty of meat.

**W**e do not know exactly how **Ceratosaurus** hunted. It may have done so on its own, hiding behind trees and then jumping on its prey.

**S**ome scientists, however, think that **Ceratosaurus** may have hunted in small packs, like wolves. Two or three dinosaurs could have brought down a much bigger animal than just one dinosaur hunting alone.

**W**hen **Ceratosaurus** attacked prey – such as the young **Camarasaurus** (KAM-<u>AR</u>-A-<u>SAW</u>-RUS) shown here – it may have first dug its teeth into the animal.

Then, using powerful neck muscles, it would rip pieces of flesh from its victim.

**Ceratosaurus** may also have used its strong arms to hold the prey down. But, like many other carnivores, **Ceratosaurus** may also have eaten the remains of animals it found lying around on the ground.

So it could have been a scavenger as well.

**But** how did **Ceratosaurus** manage to swallow huge chunks of meat? From its skeleton, we know that the skull was built to expand sideways, so that its jaws could open very wide.

**Ceratosaurus** would certainly have been able to swallow most of *you* in one gulp! (But, of course, no humans existed at this time.)

# Horned fighter

Two male **Ceratosaurus** faced each other. They roared loudly and waved their tails in anger. The two were obviously enemies and ready to fight over something.

One of the two furious creatures gave a threatening snort that echoed all around. It wanted to show how powerful it was and scare its rival. They both wanted the female for a mate.

**B**ut what could their argument have been about? Why were they so angry with each other? It was the mating season, and these two male bullies were fighting over a female.

The other rose to the challenge and lowered its head, ready to charge at its opponent. A dreadful battle was about to begin. Now they both gave a terrifying roar, each trying to outdo the other with the noises they made. What would happen next?

14

Whack! Whack! The two male **Ceratosaurus** battered each other with the horns on their noses. Again and again they collided, using the sharp, bony ridges over their eyes as weapons, too.

Whack! Whack! Meanwhile, the female they were fighting over waited nervously in the distance.

On and on they fought, their horned noses getting battered every time their heads collided.

Eventually, it all became too much for the weaker dinosaur of this rival pair. He was tired and decided nothing – not even the female **Ceratosaurus** – was worth such a bashing. He had had enough.

There was no way she could stop them fighting over her. Anyway, she wanted to mate with the stronger of the two **Ceratosaurus**. Which one would prove to be the most powerful?

Slowly, he turned around and stalked away. What a headache he had! It had all been too much.

His rival would now court the waiting female. As for the loser, he would feel better tomorrow and try again for a different mate.

15

# Dinosaur footprints

Dinosaurs have been extinct for many millions of years. But we can still learn a lot about these animals from their skeletons and from the footprints they left.

By studying the footprints of dinosaurs, scientists can tell whether they walked on two or four legs, how many toes they had, if they had claws, and how big the creatures were.

**Ceratosaurus**, for example, once roamed the muddy banks of rivers in the eastern foothills of the Rocky Mountains. Their footprints remained in the mud, which slowly hardened. The prints have been preserved in a wide stretch of rocks many miles long that is also rich in dinosaur bones.

Scientists can even tell how fast the dinosaurs moved. They do this by measuring the distance between prints and the depth of the prints. If there are many similar prints together, with smaller ones in the middle, it is likely the dinosaurs were traveling in groups, younger ones walking on the inside, protected by the adults.

The best prints come from giant dinosaurs like **Diplodocus**. Some of their prints are nearly as long as you are tall.

# Great Ceratosaurus mysteries

Other bones that have been found, however, point to it having been a lot longer.

Experts are still not certain about the horn on **Ceratosaurus**'s snout. As you have seen on previous pages, it was probably used to butt rival males. Or it may have been very large on males in order to impress the females.

The bony ridges above the eyes provide another riddle. They, too, could also have been used in fights or to show off to the females.

We have a fairly good idea what **Ceratosaurus** looked like. But some things are still a mystery.

For instance, how did it hunt? Some scientists think it hunted in packs.

And what about its size? Some skeletons show that the animal was about 20 feet (6 m) long.

A narrow row of bony plates ran along **Ceratosaurus**'s back. These stood up like a low ridge. No one is quite sure what the purpose of this ridge was. It doesn't seem big enough to have protected this dinosaur against enemies. Perhaps it was a sort of ornament to help one **Ceratosaurus** recognize another of its own kind.

If more skeletons of **Ceratosaurus** are discovered by paleontologists, such puzzles may be solved.

# Ceratosaurus data

**Ceratosaurus**, as we have seen, was a fierce, two-legged meat-eater with a long, thick tail. Let's take a look at different parts of its body again. In many ways, it was similar to the giant carnivore **Allosaurus**. But **Ceratosaurus** was only about half its size.

These neck muscles also gave **Ceratosaurus** the strength to tear flesh from its unfortunate victims.

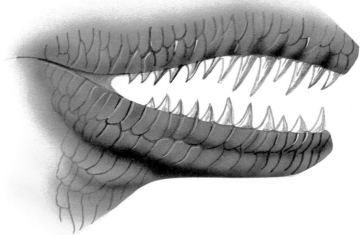

### Curved teeth

As it was a carnivore, **Ceratosaurus** needed big, sharp teeth to bite at its prey and rip off the meat. Like other large hunters, **Ceratosaurus**'s teeth curved back into its large mouth. This meant that when **Ceratosaurus** held its prey between its teeth, the victim could struggle as much as it might, but would find escape almost impossible.

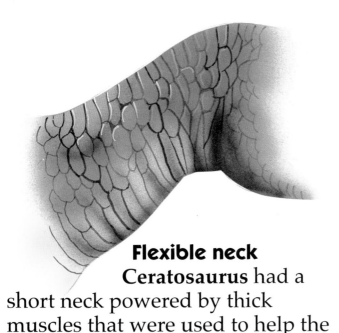

### Flexible neck

**Ceratosaurus** had a short neck powered by thick muscles that were used to help the neck move from side to side.

## Horned snout

On the top of its snout, unlike **Allosaurus**, **Ceratosaurus** had a large, bony horn. The males probably used the horn when fighting over a mate. The horn may have been designed to attract females in the mating season, too. Its size may also have shown others the age of the dinosaur.

## Strong claws

**Ceratosaurus** had large, strong toe claws. The first toe pointed backward and cannot be seen here.

## Four-fingered hands

**Ceratosaurus** had small hands, each of which had four fingers, as you can see below. This was quite unusual, since other large meat-eaters of Late Jurassic times – **Allosaurus**, for example – had hands with only three fingers.

Having an extra finger must have helped to give **Ceratosaurus** a better grip on its prey.

**Allosaurus** and **Ceratosaurus** were both large carnivores, living at the same time in the same part of the world. But how were they different? From what you have discovered while reading this book, you should now know how to tell them apart.

# Meet some other carnivores

Most meat-eating (carnivorous) dinosaurs, like **Ceratosaurus** (**1**), were large and heavily built. They had great heads with fearsome jaws, and their necks were short and powerful.

**Dryptosaurus** (<u>DRIP</u>-TOE-<u>SAW</u>-RUS) (**2**), for example, lived in Cretaceous times and prowled around that part of the world we now call North America. Its arms were quite strong with sharp claws.

Scientists think that, at more than 20 feet (6 m) long and about twice the height of a grown man, **Dryptosaurus** could have leapt out on fairly large dinosaurs, killing them for food.

**Staurikosaurus** (STOR-IK-OH-SAW-RUS) (**3**) was from North and South America but lived in earlier Triassic times. It was much smaller than most meat-eaters at only 6.5 feet (2 m) long and just twice the height of a domestic cat. But it had large teeth for tearing flesh.

**Staurikosaurus** could also run very fast on long legs, so it was probably a successful predator.

**Spinosaurus** (SPINE-OH-SAW-RUS) (**4**) – another fearsome **Carnosaur** – lived during the Cretaceous Period about 110 million years ago in what are now the African countries of Niger and Egypt.

This dinosaur was huge, measuring up to 40 feet (12 m) long. Just look at how much bigger than **Ceratosaurus** it was!

The most striking thing about **Spinosaurus** was the sail on its back. This was made of skin held up by spines that stood as high as a tall man does today. The sail may have been used to control the dinosaur's body temperature.

All these carnivores were forever on the lookout for food and would never have gone hungry for long!

**3**

# GLOSSARY

**carnivores** — meat-eating animals.

**extinction** — the dying out of all members of a plant or animal species.

**mate** (v) — to join together (animals) to produce young.

**pack** — a group of similar or related animals.

**paleontologists** — scientists who study the remains of plants and animals that lived millions of years ago.

**predators** — animals that capture and kill other animals for food.

**prey** — an animal that is killed for food by another animal.

**remains** — a skeleton, bones, or a dead body.

**scavenger** — any animal that eats dead or decaying matter.

**snout** — protruding nose and jaws of an animal.

# INDEX

**Allosaurus** 9, 11, 20, 21

**Camarasaurus** 12
carnivores 21, 22-23
**Carnosaur** 23
**Ceratosaurus**: as carnivore 5, 7, 9, 12-13, 20, 22; claws of 7, 21; eye ridges of 5, 6, 8, 15, 19; four-fingered hands of 5, 7, 21; hips of 9; horned snout of 5, 6, 8, 9, 15, 19, 21; and mating 14, 15, 21; physical characteristics of 6, 7, 19; powerful jaws of 7, 9, 13; powerful legs of 9; remains of 8, 9; ridged back of 5, 7, 9, 19; as scavenger 13; sharp teeth of 7, 20; short arms of 7; short neck of 9, 12; skeleton of 9, 13, 19; skull of 9, 13; tail of 7
conifers 10
Cretaceous Period 22, 23
cycads 10

**Diplodocus** 11, 17
**Dryptosaurus** 22, 23

extinct 17

Felch, M. P. 8

Jurassic Period 7, 10-11, 21

Marsh, O. C. 6
mud banks 11

**Ornitholestes** 11

packs 12, 19
paleontologists 6, 8, 19
plains 7, 10
plant-eaters 11
predator 23
prey 7, 12, 20, 21

quarry 8

remains 12

scavenger 13
scientists 8, 9, 10, 12, 17, 19, 23
**Spinosaurus** 23
**Staurikosaurus** 23
**Stegosaurus** 11

Triassic Period 23